THE LANTERN BEARERS SERIES

When the night is darkest, there are always those who hold up a lantern to light the way.

Book 1: The Lamp of Education

The Winter Plum: How Wu Yifang Became the First Woman to Sign the UN Charter

From bound feet in 1893 China to the United Nations in 1945, Wu Yifang bloomed like a winter plum—fearless in frost, fragrant and strong. She became China's first female PhD in Biology, led Ginling College through World War II, and became the first woman to sign the UN Charter. Her lamp of education lit the way for generations.

Book 2: The Lamp of Compassion

The Sheltering Tree: How Minnie Vautrin Saved 10,000 Lives in Wartime China

When darkness fell on Nanjing in 1937, Minnie Vautrin became a sheltering tree, her branches wide enough to protect ten thousand women and children. The "Goddess of Nanking" stood between soldiers and refugees, risking her life daily. Her lamp of compassion burned through the darkest nights.

Book 3: The Lamp of Truth

The Iris Blooms: How Iris Chang Revealed the Truth About the Nanjing Massacre

Like the iris flower—her namesake—Iris Chang bloomed in defiance, revealing truths the world had forgotten. Her groundbreaking book *The Rape of Nanking* (1997) broke sixty years of silence and awakened global awareness. Her lamp of truth continues to shine, reminding us that memory is an act of justice.

Three women. Three flowers. Three lamps. Together, they prove that even a single flame can drive away the darkness.
May their light inspire you to be brave, to be kind, and to stand for truth.

The Winter Plum

How Wu Yifang Became the First Woman to Sign the UN Charter

Written by
TAN FENGXIA

Illustrated by
WANG ZUMIN

RC
Books Beyond Boundaries
ROYAL COLLINS

The Winter Plum: How Wu Yifang Became the First Woman to Sign the UN Charter

Book 1 of *The Lantern Bearers Series*

Writer: Tan Fengxia
Acquisitions editor: Yu Xiaohua
Illustrator: Wang Zumin
Translators: Daniel Jingyuan Ni and Xuemeng Angela Li

First published in 2026 by Royal Collins Publishing Group Inc.
Groupe Publication Royal Collins Inc.
550-555 boul. René-Lévesque O Montréal (Québec) H2Z1B1 Canada

10 9 8 7 6 5 4 3 2 1

Originally published in Chinese as《教育之灯：吴贻芳的故事》

ISBN: 978-1-4878-1389-5

To find out more about our publications, please visit www.royalcollins.com.

"Women should be like the Winter Plum—strong bones, sweet fragrance, needing no spring wind to bloom."

—WU YIFANG

Winter, 1893. Wuchang, China.

In the frozen courtyard, Winter Plum blossoms danced in the frost—small, but fearless.

Inside the warm house, a baby girl was born.

"We shall call her Dong'er," Grandmother whispered. "Child of Winter."

But Father looked at the brave blossoms outside. He gave her a name that carried the scent of flowers and the strength of virtue: Wu Yifang.

Yifang watched her brothers pack for school.

"Why can't I go?" she asked.

"The world outside is not for girls," they said.

She looked at her feet, bound tight in cloth. She looked at the snow-covered walls. She felt like a bird in a cage.

"It isn't fair," she told the falling snow. "We all have minds."

When Yifang was eleven, hope arrived: a girls' school was opening!

She begged her father until his heart softened.

"Go," he said.

The heavy gates opened. Yifang and her sister stepped out of the courtyard and into the world.

They were no longer birds in a cage.

They were free.

School was a garden of wonders.

The sisters learned English, Mathematics, Music, and the secrets of nature. They devoured every book like hungry birds.

Through the window, they watched wild birds soaring.

"One day," they dreamed, "our wings will be strong enough to fly like them."

But winter storms strike without warning. In one month, the light went out.
Father. Brother. Mother. Sister ... all gone.
Yifang stood alone in the dark, drowning in grief. "Why go on?" she cried.
Her uncle's voice cut through the shadows: "Look at your little sister. She needs you. Living takes courage."
Yifang lifted her head.

With her uncle's support, Yifang found her path.

She traveled to Beijing. The train passed ancient city walls.

But she could not just be a student. She became a teacher of English, working to support her grandmother and raise her little sister.

She was no longer a child. She was her family's protector.

The Winter Plum blooms stronger each year.

In 1916, a former teacher saw Yifang's talent and recommended her to Ginling College.

Yifang walked through the gate with her suitcase and a dream.

She didn't know it yet, but this school would become her heart, her home, her destiny.

By day, Yifang studied hard. At night, she held her family photo tight. The moonlight caught her tears.

Her classmate Xu Yizhen noticed her silence and reached out.

When Xu learned of Yifang's tragedy, she was shocked. "To carry such pain and still study so hard—you are truly strong!"

They became soulmates, exploring their faith together and making a promise: to serve society.

Yifang was elected President of the Student Council. Then, in 1919, the May Fourth Movement erupted.

Graduation exams were coming, but Yifang made a bold choice. “We will delay our graduation,” she told her classmates. “The fate of the nation concerns everyone. We cannot stay silent.”

She led fifty girls into the streets to protest. They organized classes to teach women and children to read, spreading the spirit of patriotism.

金陵女大
天下興亡
匹夫有責
鹽水鴨

Ginling's teachers were the best of the best.

It was a time when new ideas about democracy and science were sweeping China.

Yifang fell in love with Chemistry and Biology. While others rested, she buried herself in the laboratory, exploring the magic of science.

The first graduating class had only five students.

At twenty-six, Wu Yifang was the brightest star.

They became the first women to receive bachelor's degrees on Chinese soil.

Yifang accepted her diploma from Mrs. Thurston, fighting back tears.

"If only Father, Mother, Brother, and Sister were here to see this day."

After graduation, a new path opened: a scholarship to the University of Michigan for a PhD in Biology.

Yifang said goodbye to her grandmother. She didn't know it would be their final farewell.

In America, she worked harder than ever. Her professor called her the most brilliant student he'd ever seen.

When news of the May Thirtieth Movement reached them, she rallied Chinese students to raise funds and protest.

"China has a glorious history!" she proclaimed. "We must make our nation strong again!"

Even far from home, Yifang defended China's dignity.

In 1926, Australia's Prime Minister visited Michigan. In his speech, he insulted China. Yifang stood up immediately. "This is slander!" she cried, walking out in protest.

That night, she wrote a fierce rebuttal. It was published in *The Michigan Daily* the next morning.

Her courage won deep respect.

Five years passed. Yifang was writing her doctoral thesis.

The Michigan winter was freezing. She missed the Winter Plum's fragrance from home.

Then a letter arrived: Ginling's Board invited her to return as President!

Yifang replied, "If the school needs me urgently, I will give up my degree and come home. But I dare not accept the title of president—my heart is in science."

The Board was moved. "Finish your degree first. Then come lead us."

In 1928, Yifang graduated with honors—China's first female PhD in Zoology.

On the ship home, her heart raced with the waves.

She made a promise to the ocean: "I will dedicate my life to my country and to the education of women."

The Ginling campus welcomed its brilliant daughter home.
On November 3, 1928, Yifang solemnly accepted the school seal.
She announced her mission:
"We are here to create women leaders who will be of use to society."

President Wu cherished the school motto: “Abundant Life.” She taught: “Life’s purpose is not to live only for oneself. Use your wisdom to help others. This makes your life fuller.”

Beside her stood Dean Minnie Vautrin. From that day, they became inseparable partners.

Visitors called Ginling "The most beautiful campus in the Orient."

President Wu knew education's heart lay in its teachers. She set three rules: "First, have a true interest in students. Second, have true knowledge. Most importantly, have a noble character to be a model for youth."

The college felt like a family.

Yifang believed in "Whole Person Education."

Students studied both Arts and Science. They played sports, made music, and learned home economics.

Her goal: raise women with self-respect, self-reliance, and self-confidence.

Under her care, Ginling grew like a great tree—filling the world with fragrance.

Summer 1937. War clouds gathered.
Yifang rallied the women of Nanjing: "Our soldiers are freezing."
Needles flashed. They sewed thousands of winter coats for the warriors.
Education was important.
But survival came first.

July 7, 1937. Japan invaded China.

Yifang was invited to a government meeting in Lushan. But she did more than talk.

With Minnie Vautrin, she organized students to sew warm coats for wounded soldiers.

On Founder's Day, they sent a telegram to every Ginling branch: "We must shoulder the national crisis. We must be worthy of our ideals."

"Abundant Life" now meant: give your life for the country.

War closed in on Nanjing. The school could not stay.
Minnie chose to guard the campus. Yifang would lead students west.
They said a heavy goodbye—two branches of the same Winter Plum tree.
One staying to weather the storm.
One carrying the seeds to new soil.

The escape was a nightmare.

Air raid sirens screamed.

Yifang led her students to the docks, hearts pounding. Suddenly—Japanese planes dove. Bombs fell like rain into the Yangtze River.

Students wept, but Yifang stood firm. "China needs education to become strong. We will guard this fortress of learning at all costs."

Yifang made a bold decision: move the school to Chengdu, to join West China Union University.

Students trekked through mountains, singing to drown out fear.

On their first night, there were no beds. They slept on the rough floor. Yifang ate the same simple food and slept beside them. They faced hardship together.

Even in war, standards remained high.

Eve Curie, daughter of Marie Curie, visited as a war correspondent. She praised their dance class as "heroic."

A British reporter photographed students practicing archery. He called them "The Wartime Mulans."

This photo appeared on *LIFE Magazine*'s cover, showing the world the brave spirit of Chinese women.

Bombs still fell on Chengdu.

Yifang told her students, “Wake up your spirits! Recognize your mission!”

The students formed a “Wartime Service Corps.”

President Wu stood with them, supporting their work to save the nation.

They formed an Air Raid Rescue Squad. Yifang worked beside them.

At midnight, after the sirens stopped, she gently bandaged the wounded. “If we work together, victory will be ours.”

In the corner, she placed Winter Plum blossoms inside an empty artillery shell. The fragrance drove away the smell of death.

Yifang had no children, but she mothered every poor child she met. She opened clinics, nurseries, and free schools for war orphans.

Wherever Ginling went, "Abundant Life" followed. Students taught farmers to read and mothers to care for babies.

Yifang's feet had been bound in childhood—deformed and painful. Yet on these feet, she walked miles over mountains to visit students, inspiring everyone she met.

Though safe in Chengdu, their hearts were in occupied Nanjing.

News came of the horrific Nanjing Massacre.

Yifang learned that Minnie and colleagues were guarding the campus, sheltering thousands of women and children. She felt deep respect, but also burning anxiety.

She wished she could be there to help.

By 1941, the Pacific War broke out. The Japanese seized the Nanjing campus.

On the school anniversary, President Wu acted in a play called *The Autobiography of Ginling* to ignite patriotism.

Listening to the bell in Chengdu, they missed the clear chime of Nanjing.

They missed the Winter Plums that filled their old home with fragrance.

The war had taught her one truth: World peace requires everyone.

In 1943, Yifang traveled to the US as one of the "Six Professors" to tell China's story.

Her speeches were powerful. Smith College honored her with a Doctor of Laws.

In June, she stood in Constitution Hall in Washington, DC, her voice ringing out for justice and freedom.

March 1944. Yifang returned.

Students sang on the lawn: "Listen to the bells … Welcome Wu Yifang, bringing glory to our people."

While in America, it was her 50th birthday. Alumni raised money for a gift. But Yifang wouldn't spend it on herself. She brought it back to improve teachers' meals.

Her love was like spring rain—silent, but giving life.

"Men have Cai Yuanpei. Women have Wu Yifang." She was a legend.

April 1945. San Francisco. The United Nations Conference.

When China's turn came, Yifang stood calm and elegant. In fluent English, she spoke of China's eight-year fight against aggression. She called for the world to unite for peace.

Her wisdom and grace won thunderous applause.

China was the first nation to sign the UN Charter.

Wu Yifang became the first woman to sign her name on this "cornerstone of peace." Her name is etched in history forever.

That same day, she sent a telegram to the 1945 graduates: "History turns a new page today. The future depends on whether you can sacrifice the small self for the highest ideal."

Reading her words, the students pledged to follow in her footsteps.

Finally, dawn broke! Japan surrendered.
In Chengdu, teachers and students sang the school song with tears and laughter.
In 1946, they returned to Nanjing.
But the city was scarred. The campus was quiet. Minnie Vautrin was gone.
Yifang held a memorial service, deeply mourning her friend.

Yifang led Ginling for 23 years. She "married" the school and became the "Mother of Ginling."

Decades later, she could still name every student.

In 1979, at age 86, she returned to Michigan to receive the "Wisdom Goddess Award." Surrounded by her successful students, she smiled under the golden ginkgo trees.

Her belief remained unchanged: "Women should be like the Winter Plum—strong bones, sweet fragrance, needing no spring wind to bloom."

Words to Know

Bound Feet
A painful ancient Chinese practice where girls' feet were tightly wrapped to keep them small. Wu Yifang's feet were bound when she was young, but she refused to let this stop her from walking her own path.

Ginling College
The first college in China to grant bachelor's degrees to women. Wu Yifang studied here and later became its president for 23 years.

May Fourth Movement
A student-led protest in China demanding democracy, science, and justice. Wu Yifang and her classmates marched in the streets to fight for their country's future.

Cai Yuanpei
China's "Father of Modern Education" and former president of Peking University. He fought to open education to women and promoted science and democracy in China. When people said, "Men have Cai Yuanpei. Women have Wu Yifang," they meant Wu Yifang was as great a leader in women's education as Cai was for all of China.

PhD
Doctor of Philosophy—the highest level of education in a subject. Wu Yifang became the first Chinese woman to earn a PhD in Biology.

United Nations Charter
The founding document of the United Nations, signed in 1945 to promote world peace. Wu Yifang was the first woman to sign it, representing China.

"Abundant Life"
Ginling College's motto, meaning: "The purpose of life is not to live only for yourself, but to use your gifts to help others."

Nanjing Massacre
A tragic event (1937–1938) during World War II, when many innocent people in Nanjing suffered. Minnie Vautrin and others worked to protect survivors.

The Journey of Wu Yifang (1893–1985)

A Life Dedicated to Education and Peace

1893 Born on January 26 in Wuchang, China. Her father named her "Yifang," meaning "Fragrance of Virtue."

1916 Entered Ginling College. Rose to become Student Council President.

1919 Led fellow students in the May Fourth Movement protests, fighting for China's future.

1928 Earned her PhD in Biology from the University of Michigan. Returned to China to become the President of Ginling College.

1937 During WWII, led students on a difficult journey west to Chengdu to keep the school running.

1945 Became the first woman to sign the United Nations Charter in San Francisco.

1979 Received the "Wisdom Goddess Award" from the University of Michigan.

1985 Passed away in Nanjing on November 10. Her legacy lives on in every student she inspired.

Selected Bibliography

Cheng, Sihui, and Sun Haiying. *A Model for Women: Wu Yifang, President of Ginling College*. Jinan: Shandong Education Press, 2004.

Hu, Hua-Ling. *American Goddess at the Rape of Nanking: The Courage of Minnie Vautrin*. Carbondale: Southern Illinois University Press, 2000.

Zhou, Heping. *Forever Wu Yifang: In Commemoration of Her 120th Birthday*. Nanjing: Jiangsu People's Publishing House, 2013.

About the Author

TAN FENGXIA is a Hans Christian Andersen Award Juror (2024, 2026) and Professor of Children's Literature at Nanjing Normal University, China.

As one of the world's leading scholars of children's books, she has devoted her career to bringing Chinese stories to young readers everywhere. She has been a research fellow at Cambridge University and the International Youth Library in Munich.

The Winter Plum is her tribute to the brave women of Nanjing—the city where she has lived and taught for decades, walking the same paths Wu Yifang once walked.

Tan Fengxia believes every child deserves to see themselves as a hero of history.

About the Illustrator

WANG ZUMIN is one of China's most celebrated picture book artists. His work has been honored at the Bologna Children's Book Fair and has won the Chen Bochui International Children's Literature Award.

For *The Winter Plum*, Wang created over forty original watercolor paintings, bringing to life the frost-covered courtyards of 1890s China, the brave faces of wartime students, and the historic moment when Wu Yifang's pen touched the UN Charter.

His art has been featured in national exhibitions across China and has touched the hearts of millions of young readers.